Nana, What's Cancer?

Nana, What's Cancer?

Written by
Beverlye Hyman Fead and Tessa Mae Hamermesh

Illustrated by
Shennen Bersani

American Cancer Society®

Published by the American Cancer Society
Health Promotions
250 Williams Street NW
Atlanta, GA 30303-1002

Manufactured by Dickinson Press Inc.
Manufactured in Grand Rapids, MI, in July 2010
Job # 3745400

Printed in the United States of America

6 5 4 3 2 10 11 12 13 14

Library of Congress Cataloging-in-Publication Data
Fead, Beverlye Hyman.
Nana, what's cancer?/Beverlye Hyman Fead and Tessa Mae Hamermesh.
   p. cm.
 Includes bibliographical references.
 ISBN-13: 978-1-60443-010-3 (hardcover: alk. paper)
 ISBN-10: 1-60443-010-9 (hardcover: alk. paper)
 1. Cancer—Juvenile literature. I. Hamermesh, Tessa Mae. II. Title.

RC264.F43 2009
616.99'4—dc22   2009002094

American Cancer Society
Strategic Director, Content: Chuck Westbrook
Director, Cancer Information: Terri Ades, DNP, FNP-BC, AOCN
Director, Book Publishing: Len Boswell
Managing Editor, Books: Rebecca Teaff, MA
Books Editor: Jill Russell
Book Publishing Coordinator: Vanika Jordan, MSPub
Editorial Assistant, Books: Amy Rovere

Book Development by
Bookhouse Group, Inc.
818 Marietta Street NW
Atlanta, GA 30318
404-885-9515
bookhouse.net

Editorial Director: Rob Levin
Managing Editor: Renee Peyton
Book and Cover Designer: Matthew Jeffirs

For more information about cancer, contact your American Cancer Society at **800-227-2345** or on the Web at **cancer.org**.

Quantity discounts on bulk purchases of this book are available. Book excerpts can also be created to fit specific needs. For information, please contact the American Cancer Society, Health Promotions Publishing, 250 Williams Street NW, Atlanta, GA 30303-1002, or send an e-mail to **trade.sales@cancer.org**.

For special sales, contact us at trade.sales@cancer.org.

From Nana and Tess

To Gideon and Alexander Hyman,
twin grandsons of Beverlye and cousins of Tess

Our wish for them and future generations is to live in a
cancer-free—at least a cancer-*controlled*—world.

And to the scientists and doctors who will help make this possible.

From Shennen

My heartfelt thanks to Jack Monchik, MD, for making me a cancer survivor.

Contents

1   Nana, what's cancer? 1

2   What causes cancer? 5

3   Can you catch cancer? 9

4   Can anyone get cancer? 13

5   When you have cancer, do you have to stay in bed? 15

6   Can you get cancer when you already have another disease? . . 19

7   Is it okay to feel sad when someone you love has cancer? 23

8   Why are some cancers worse than others? 27

9   Do animals ever get cancer? 31

10   Is there anything else we can do to stop cancer? 33

11   Do children get cancer, too? 37

12   What's important to remember about cancer? 41

Resources 45

Afterwords 47

Acknowledgments 49

Glossary 51

About the Authors 54

About the Illustrator 55

"Nana, what's cancer?"

My granddaughter, Tess, and I sat in my kitchen, eating Girl Scout cookies and drinking chamomile tea. She liked the Tagalong cookies—round, chocolate-covered cookies with peanut butter in the middle. They were her favorites!

I could tell Tess had a lot on her mind. I had been having treatment for cancer, and Tess wanted to know more about it. She said she wanted to ask me some questions about **cancer***— about the things that bothered her.

"It might help if you write out your questions," I told her.

She nodded and with a look of great concentration, jotted down the first question: "What is cancer?"

"I think this is the best way to explain it," I said. "Our bodies are made up of cells that grow, divide, and die. But cancer cells don't go through this cycle. They continue to grow and divide and form new cells that are **abnormal**—these cells act

*For explanation of terms in bold, see page 51.

differently than normal cells. Cancer starts when the abnormal cells clump together in a person's body and form a **tumor**."

"But, Nana, what is a tumor?" she asked.

Of course, I thought, she wouldn't know the meaning of that word, so I said, "From now on, when we don't know what a word means, let's look it up.

"A tumor is a swelling or mass of **tissue** in the body. Tissues are groups of cells that have a specific job to do.

"There are two kinds of tumors: **benign** and **malignant**. Benign tumors are not cancer. They may grow larger, but they do not spread to other places in the body. But malignant tumors *are* **cancerous**. They contain abnormal cells. That's because cancer causes cells in the body to change and grow out of control."

Tess thought for a moment, and then asked, "Those bad cells spread, don't they?"

"Yes, they can enter the bloodstream and travel to different parts of the body. When the cancer spreads, it can destroy the body's healthy tissues. Healthy cells usually keep themselves under control, but unhealthy cells multiply.

"Now, it's time to use your imagination. Do you want to show an example of what we mean and draw a group of tennis balls? And then, imagine those tennis balls as tumors?"

"Yes, that would be easy, Nana! First, I'll draw the normal ones together, and then the abnormal ones that grow apart and spread."

"Great," I said. "That makes it easier to understand."

"What causes cancer?"

Later that afternoon, Tess and I decided to go to a movie. On the way to the theater we listened to Louis Armstrong singing "Cheek to Cheek." I had played that song for her in the car since she was a baby.

Tess was singing along, "Heaven, I'm in heaven." Then she stopped and said, "Nana, there's something else I want to ask you."

"Sure," I answered. "Ask away."

"What actually causes cancer?"

"Tess, we don't always know exactly what causes a person's cancer, but we do know that cancer occurs because of certain interactions between **genetics**, **environment**, and **behavior**."

"What do those words mean, and why are they so important? Do they apply to everyone?" Tess asked.

"Yes, they do. Genetics is the study of how parents pass on certain traits to their children—like the color of our eyes and hair, as well as how tall or short we will be when we grow up. Genetics may also tell us if we'll have any serious health problems and what they might be."

Tess looked at me and said, "I know what environment means! It's our surroundings, like the air we breathe and the places we live and play."

I smiled. "That's right. Very good! And then there's behavior, which is what we do, how we act or how we react to things that happen to us—to a new situation or challenge.

"Here's another way to think about cancer," I said. "In a book called *The Guide to Fighting for Recovery from Cancer*, cancer is described as a tiger that's escaped his cage. Picture him prowling and growling right in front of you."

"That sounds too scary!"

"It doesn't have to be scary," I said, "especially if you know what to do. You may want to run away, but that won't help the situation. We want to get that tiger back into his cage!"

Tess said, "I get it! You have to try to fight the tiger."

"Of course! Can you help me think of ways to outwit him?"

"How about eating healthy food, Nana?"

"That's a good one." I smiled. "Also, taking care of your body by exercising every day."

"We are on a roll now!" Tess said.

I laughed. "And don't forget the right medical care! And you can help, too. Encourage your loved one or your friend with cancer to do everything possible to keep the tiger in the cage. The lesson here is that we can't always beat the tiger but sometimes we can put it back into its cage and prevent it from harming us."

Tess's eyes met mine, and said, "You're lucky, Nana. You've kept your tiger in the cage now for seven years. Do you know what I think helps you a lot? Laughter."

"You're right! You and I love to laugh together. It helps me feel better."

"You mean that if we tell funny jokes or riddles to our loved ones, they'll get better?"

"Not always, but it will sure make them smile and that's a good thing."

"Can you catch cancer?"

A few weeks later, Tess came to visit me in Montecito. One morning, we walked down Coast Village Road and stopped for some breakfast at our favorite place. Tess ordered a bagel with cream cheese and hot chocolate, while I had my usual oatmeal with berries.

We took our meal outside, where we could watch the bicyclists passing by. As Tess sipped her hot chocolate, she said, "Nana, there are still some things I'm wondering about. Will cancer keep you from kissing and hugging your mom or dad, your grandmother or grandfather, or anyone else you know who might have cancer? Is getting cancer like catching a cold or the chicken pox?"

"No," I said emphatically. "You can't catch cancer from someone you love, or even from a total stranger. Cancer only happens inside the body of the person who is sick with the disease. It cannot be passed from one person to another.

"In fact, if someone you love has cancer, it's actually good to give that person lots of hugs and kisses because it will make him feel better. Also, you don't need to worry about drinking from a cup or glass that belongs to a cancer patient, or cuddling up with him or her to watch a movie, or sitting in that person's lap and reading. Isn't that good news?"

"That *is* good news, Nana! But how do people know if they have cancer?" Tess had that serious look on her face once again.

I wanted to ease her fears. "Well, first of all," I said, "a doctor figures out whether a person has cancer. When the doctor identifies what is wrong, it's called the **diagnosis**."

"The diagnosis happens after the doctor does some tests and examines a patient, right?" Tess asked.

"Yes," I said. "The doctor will study the person's **symptoms**, too. When the diagnosis is cancer, more tests may be done. After these tests and more visits with the doctor are completed, then the patients get their treatments.

"The doctor recommends the kind of medical treatments that will help the person with cancer get better. Now, you have a special job to do, too—a job that is almost as important as the doctor's. Give the person who has cancer all the comfort you can. You can say the words 'I love you,' or you can write something nice on a note or a card."

Tess added, "You can also send a book or make a special gift to make the person who is sick feel better."

"Can anyone get cancer?"

That evening, sometime after dinner, Tess and I sat on my bed to watch TV and have this weird snack combo that we like: Goldfish and carrots.

We were watching a show about a family whose teenage son had a mysterious illness. That got Tess to thinking. She knew a lot about my cancer experience, but she said she sometimes wondered if people of any age could get cancer. The answer was yes.

Surprised, Tess asked, "You mean anyone? From little kids to moms and dads and old people?"

"That's right. There are no age limits for cancer, but there's something you should remember about who gets cancer. The most important thing is that the average age of a cancer patient is sixty-six years."

She couldn't hide her smile. "Kids think that's really old."

I grinned at her. "And we both know it's not, don't we?"

She laughed. "Well, you're not old, Nana. That's for sure."

"Do you remember our trip to Washington, D.C.?"

"Yes, it was cool."

I agreed. "At the American Cancer Society's Celebration on the Hill™, we saw that cancer patients and cancer **survivors** come from every age group, from every race, and from every walk of life. We saw babies in strollers, elderly people in wheelchairs, and all the ages in between, and every one of them wore what?" I prompted.

"Survivor T-shirts," Tess supplied.

"Because…?"

"Because they all have survived cancer!"

"Right you are, Tess."

"When you have cancer, do you have to stay in bed?"

A week after our visit, Tess came down with a cold, so I went over to her house to provide some TLC with my homemade chicken soup. I found her in her room, propped up with pillows and surrounded by books.

"Nana," Tess said proudly, "I just read a book about two little girls whose mom had breast cancer. Their mom felt so sick from the treatment that she had to stay in bed. Did that happen to you?"

I smiled and said, "No, I was lucky. I needed to stay in bed only at the beginning, because of some procedures I had right after my cancer was diagnosed. Now, I take a pill and get a shot, and I lead a normal life. Sometimes people with cancer can go on with their lives, just like before. They don't have to stay in bed. They go to school or to their jobs, or just live happily with their families.

However, treatments can make people feel sick; then, they have to stay in bed until they feel better."

"So the treatments can make you feel sick?" Tess asked.

"They can, but not always. Everyone is different," I said. "Two of these treatments are **radiation** and **chemotherapy**. But there are also new chemotherapy treatments that don't cause sickness."

Tess said knowingly, "I've heard that some people have **surgery**. What happens then?"

"Then, they do have to be in bed while they heal," I answered. "They have to listen to the doctor and do whatever he or she says. The doctor might tell them to walk a little every day after surgery because that will make them get stronger. And he might say to get a lot of rest. Rest and exercise are really important for a cancer patient."

Tess nodded in agreement. "Do people with cancer sleep a lot?"

"Sometimes they do. Cancer and its treatments can tire a person out," I explained. "The combination of resting and getting some exercise is really the best thing for many people with cancer.

They might prefer to take a stroll and breathe some fresh air with you. You should ask someone with cancer if he or she would be more comfortable in bed. Tell your friend or loved one to be honest with you."

Tess seemed excited. "I think I know how I could help. I could read with my friend. Or I could get my mom to help me by renting some movies to take over, or by baking something. That would make me feel very good about what I did."

"Can you get cancer when you already have another disease?"

One day, when Tess was feeling a lot better, I suggested we go to a bookstore and do some browsing. We ended up briefly in the medical books section where there were books on all types of diseases, including cancer. Tess pointed to one of the books about cancer and said, "These books remind me of something I've been meaning to ask you. Can people who already have a disease still get cancer?"

"Yes, unfortunately you can get cancer even if you have another disease," I told Tess.

I went on to explain, "Let's say your Uncle John has heart disease. He takes medicine for it and is doing fine."

"So, can he still get cancer?"

"Yes, he can. In fact, some elderly people get cancer in their eighties and nineties,

when they already have other diseases like **heart disease** or **diabetes**."

Tess shook her head and said, "I'm definitely going to have to look in the dictionary to find out what those words mean!"

"That's a good idea," I said.

"The best advice I can give is that we have to take very good care of ourselves, no matter what we get. If we are in good health, we can better fight any disease or illness. You know all of the good things to do, right?"

"I sure do!" Tess said enthusiastically. "Exercise and eat green vegetables. What else, Nana?"

"Drink lots of water. Eat fewer high-fat foods. Use sun protection every day. Avoid **x-rays** if you don't need them—of course, you *should* get an x-ray if you have a broken bone. Avoid as much stress as possible. Don't smoke. And drink alcohol only in moderation."

Tess looked shocked and said, "Nana, kids don't smoke or drink alcohol!"

"Yes, I know that," I said sheepishly. "But it's important to hear this when you are young so you will start your good habits early."

"Is it okay to feel sad when someone you love has cancer?"

As an artist, I spend a lot of time in my studio. Sometimes, Tess and my grandsons come up to visit and paint with me. One day, when Tess was with me in the studio, I noticed that she was a little quiet. She had just found out her grandfather's (Papa Lew's) lung cancer had come back. "It's only natural to feel sad, Tess," I said. "After all, someone you love or care about is not feeling well. That's why cancer is often called a family disease."

"Why would you say that, Nana?" asked Tess.

"Because cancer affects everyone in the family," I answered. "It's natural to feel angry, disappointed, and sad. You may even feel like you could have caused the cancer in some way. But remember, people don't cause cancer.

"It's okay to cry if you need to," I told her. "We don't like to tell our friends that someone in our

family has cancer. But maybe it would help to tell someone, and then you wouldn't feel so frustrated, scared, and alone. If you share bad news with a friend, afterward your friend might say something nice to make you feel better.

"Here are some other things you can do," I said, pulling out a pen and note pad to make a list.

"Be sure to tell one or both of your parents how you feel. They can reassure you that you didn't cause this illness. Also, you will feel better if you talk about your feelings.

"Tell a friend or a teacher who may be able to understand your feelings. People want to help. They know it's too hard to go through it alone.

"Don't feel guilty about continuing your activities. Being active will make you feel better, and your friend or family member with cancer wants you to live your life as you normally would.

"Talk with your parents about how your daily routines may change. This may happen when someone in your family or a close friend is ill. Find out as much as you can about schedules and activities that might change.

"Talk to a doctor or a counselor. They're trained to help and have seen many people who are sad or scared."

"What else can we do, Nana?" Tess said.

"It's nice to ask how you can help the person who is sick. Greeting cards, phone calls, and visits can cheer a cancer patient. What else do you think would help?" I asked.

Tess smiled. "Writing down your feelings or drawing pictures helps a lot, too!"

"Why are some cancers worse than others?"

We were together in a restaurant. Tess had a Limonata, and I had sparkling water. The last few months, Tess had been very sad about her grandfather. He had had lung cancer, one of the toughest cancers there is. Sadly, he had passed away.

Tess wanted to know why some people do well with cancer and others do not. "There are all kinds of cancers and different treatments for those cancers," I answered. "We don't always know why some people respond better to cancer treatment than others."

Tess asked, "But if you find out you have cancer early, can it be fixed right away with medicines and treatments?"

"Sometimes," I replied. "There's a term for finding cancer early—before it has spread. It's called **early detection**. Some cancers, however, cannot be cured, even when they are caught early. I know that's very hard to hear.

But we always want to be truthful with one another.

"The doctors work really hard on treating every type of cancer, and they try many different kinds of medicines. They try everything they can.

"Sometimes the medicine makes the people look and feel very sick. They might get thin, lose their hair, or become very pale and weak. This is scary to see, and you might feel sad when you see these changes. Sometimes people don't feel as bad as they look; other times, they do. And sometimes, after everything has been done, a patient still may not get better; unfortunately, he might even die. If this happens, remember that we carry our loved ones in our hearts forever."

Tess thought for a moment and looked down at her Limonata. I could tell she was upset. She looked back up at me and said, "Hopefully, that means the person who died will go to heaven, and we'll all see each other again."

"That is my hope, too," I nodded. I stroked her hair and pulled her close to me. "I like to think of heaven as a very beautiful place, where people who have been sick will be all healthy again. They'll be able to laugh and sleep well, and we'll be happy for them that they are there.

"It is very important to focus on the good days we have with our sick relative or friend. Call that person often and remind him how much he is loved. Then, if he has to leave us, you can always remember those days, and you can keep a photo of him in your room. Luckily, we can keep our memories forever."

"Do animals ever get Cancer?"

One afternoon, I decided it was time for Tess and me to do something fun, so I suggested we go to the pet store to look at all the adorable puppies. Looking at the animals brought up other questions for her.

"Nana," she said, "Do animals get cancer, too?"

"Animals can get many of the same kinds of cancers that humans get," I told her. "But animals can also get medicines and treatments the way humans do."

Because Tess loves all animals, she was glad to hear that animals receive special medicines for their cancers similar to those of people. She wrinkled her brow and wanted to know more: "How would we know our animals are sick?"

"The symptoms can be about the same for animals and humans," I said. "These are things to look for: a change in the pet's behavior, a loss of appetite, a lack of interest in exercise, difficulty breathing—things like that.

"Cancer does not often occur in dogs that are younger than ten years old," I said. I could see the relief in Tess's face. "If you see these symptoms in your older dog, cat, or horse, call your veterinarian. The doctor will know how to handle it. Mostly, we don't have to worry about young healthy animals. We can look forward to a long happy time to play with them."

"Like I do with Patches, Nana?"

"Yes," I said, "just like that."

"Is there anything else we can do to stop cancer?"

Tess and I were looking through a photo album of our trip to Washington, D.C., and remembering what a great time we had. On our trip, we learned about how lawmakers are trying to pass laws for more cancer research. Tess thought that was great, but she wanted to know if there was anything else we could do to help stop cancer. "I mean, what can *we* do?" she asked.

"There are lots of things we can do to help stop cancer right in its tracks," I answered emphatically.

"Finally!" said Tess. "I am ready to hear something really good."

"Well," I said, "if people would stop bad habits like smoking cigarettes, this definitely would help prevent some cancers, such as lung cancer."

Tess seemed happier upon hearing that news. "Now we're talking, Nana!

SURVIVOR

What else?"

I continued, "A few years ago, researchers told us that one third of cancers were related to poor **nutrition** and **obesity**. So, eating healthy foods and getting lots of exercise might help prevent certain cancers.

"The most important way to stop cancer is to get regular **screenings**."

"What are screenings?" Tess asked.

"These are tests," I said, "such as a **mammogram** for detecting breast cancer and a **Pap test** for finding cervical cancer. These tests should be done on a regular basis, such as every year.

"Remember when we talked about early detection?" I asked. She nodded.

"Regular screening can detect changes in the body before they become dangerous. Cancers that can be stopped by early detection and treatment account for about half of all new cancer cases.

"We can also get involved in another way. We can ask our senators and congressmen in Washington to put more money into cancer research. Children can ask their parents to show them how to write to their representatives. Sometimes, you can even reach out to them online. Every voice helps, you know.

"So, if we have regular screenings as we get older, eat good foods, play a lot of sports (which we like to do anyway), protect our skin from sun rays, and never smoke, then the **survival rate** would jump to 95 percent. Just imagine, wouldn't that be great?"

"Yes, Nana, I love that thought!"

"Do children get cancer, too?"

I picked up Tess from her school one sunny afternoon and suggested we stop for a snack on the way home. As we drove along, Tess said, "Today, my teacher talked about things kids could do to have better health. I already knew lots of information from talking to you."

Tess remembered our conversation about how cancer can affect people of all ages. "So, can children get cancer, too?" she asked.

"Children can get cancer, but it is much less common in young people than in grownups. I recently read some promising news about childhood cancer," I smiled. "Even though we hope that none of our younger friends will have to deal with cancer, it is encouraging to know that the odds of a child getting cancer by the age of nineteen are low."

"How low?" asked Tess.

"Well, in a group of 330 children, only one of them will get cancer."

HOW CAN YOU STAY HEALTHY ?

Fats, Oils, and Sweets

Milk

Proteins and Meats

Vegetables

Fruits

Grains, Breads, and Starches

EXERCISE
EAT FRUITS
VEGETABLES
DON'T SMOKE

"That sounds like a small number, Nana."

"It is. And that's only part of the good news," I said. "More and more children with cancer are surviving every year. I think that is also very hopeful! Don't you?"

Tess looked relieved and nodded. "Are there special doctors for children with cancer to go to?"

I was happy to say yes. "The doctors who treat children with cancer are called **pediatric oncologists**. These doctors have formed a group called the Children's Oncology Group. Their mission is to improve cure rates for all children with cancer. Their goal is to see the cure rate for children go up to 85 percent in the near future."

"That rocks!" Tess said.

"It sure does," I exclaimed.

"But, Nana, I'm confused about something. Do children get the same type of cancer as adults?"

"Not really. Remember that we talked about some things adults do that increase the chance of getting cancer? With children, those things are different. And so are the types of cancer they get."

"So how do you know a child has cancer?" Tess asked. "Are the symptoms the same for children as they are for adults?"

"The symptoms are often about the same for a child, a teenager, or an adult," I said. "It depends on what type of cancer the person has.

"Remember that these wonderful children's doctors make each diagnosis and take very good care of all their patients with cancer. Overall, there is a great chance that children with cancer will go through the treatment, survive, and go on with their lives. Don't forget all those kids we saw in Washington wearing their survivor T-shirts, Tess."

"I remember, Nana."

"What's important to remember about cancer?"

We were back in my kitchen again, drinking chamomile tea and eating Tess's favorite Tagalong Girl Scout cookies when she asked me another question. Perhaps this was the most important question of all: "What should we remember about cancer?"

She was a good student, I thought. "Research for cancer is happening all the time," I told her. "So we will continue to learn new things about cancer, Tess. But here are some facts to think about now:

"Poor diet and lack of physical activity are linked to cancer. So eat good food and exercise!

"Also, many cancers are caused by cigarette smoking. Smoking makes lung cancers and several other cancers more common. Smoking hurts young people's fitness, endurance, and performance in sports. So . . . no smoking!

"Remember, the number of people surviving cancer because of early detection is improving. If a person's cancer is discovered early and new and improved treatments are used to fight it, there is a very good chance that person will be a cancer survivor. Early detection is very important in certain cancers like colon cancer and breast cancer."

Tess and I had covered a lot of information about cancer. I was happy when she said, "It seems to me, Nana, that our chances of recovering from cancer are getting much better."

"I think you're right. Even though cancer is a very serious disease, new tests, medicines, and treatments are helping. And don't forget, lots of research is happening behind the scenes, so that doctors can give patients better treatments. However, there is one thing that we should never forget to do."

Tess smiled. "I know what that is, Nana—laugh."

"Yes, and remember, we can get through anything if we can laugh and love each other!"

Tess and I wrapped our arms around each other.

"I love you, Tess."

"I love you too, Nana."

—The End—

Resources

Benjamin, Harold H. *Wellness Community: Guide to Fighting for Recovery from Cancer.* New York: Jeremy P. Tarcher/Penguin, 1995.

Coleman, C. Norman. *Understanding Cancer: A Patient's Guide to Diagnosis, Prognosis, and Treatment.* Baltimore: The Johns Hopkins University Press, 1998.

Curtis, Jamie Lee. *Where Do Balloons Go? An Uplifting Mystery.* New York: HarperCollins, 2000.

Fine, Judylaine. *Afraid to Ask: A Book for Families to Share About Cancer.* New York: Lothrop, Lee & Shepard, 1986.

Grobstein, Ruth H. *The Breast Cancer Book: What You Need to Know to Make Informed Decisions.* New Haven: Yale University Press Health & Wellness, 2005.

Heiney, Sue P., Hermann, Joan F., Bruss, Katherine V., and Fincannon, Joy L. *Cancer in the Family: Helping Children Cope with a Parent's Illness.* Atlanta: American Cancer Society, 2001.

Russell, Neil. *Can I Still Kiss You? Answering Your Children's Questions About Cancer.* Deerfield Beach, FL: Health Communications, 2001.

Shriver, Maria. *What's Wrong with Timmy?* New York: Little Brown & Company and Warner Books, 2001.

Afterwords . . .

From Nana: I have been a cancer survivor for almost seven years. My diagnosis was stage IV cancer. In other words, I am living with my cancer. I was lucky enough to have been given an experimental treatment and, miraculously, have been feeling great and living a normal life ever since. The result of feeling like a miracle is that I savor each and every day and, more important, I love and appreciate the relationships I share with my wonderful husband and family.

When we began this project, my granddaughter, Tess, was an eight-year-old second grade student. Today, she's a vibrant eleven-year-old—the only girl and eldest of my five grandchildren.

After I was first diagnosed with cancer, I wrote a book called *I Can Do This: Living with Cancer, Tracing a Year of Hope.* Tess loved watching me write the book. She even attended some of my book signings and kept a copy of my book on her bedside table. When she announced to her mother that she wanted to do a book report about Nana's cancer book for her second grade class, my daughter, Terry, wisely reminded Tess that most children her age know very little about cancer and that she knew about this illness because her Nana had cancer and had written and published a book about it.

After thinking about her mother's comments, Tess asked, "Why don't Nana and I write a book that explains cancer to children?"

Terry responded, "Great, why don't you call Nana?"

For me, this was a true win–win proposition because it allowed me to work on a worthwhile project with my granddaughter and, of course, it would give us a chance to help other children understand cancer.

We hope our conversation has explained some facts about cancer and taken away some of the scariness about this disease. If you have a family member or a friend who has received a cancer diagnosis, you may use this book to help that person. The more knowledge you have, the less afraid you will be if someone close to you receives a diagnosis of cancer.

A glossary is included to help explain some words associated with cancer that may be unfamiliar to readers. There is also a list of books that can help.

Thank you for joining our conversation!

From Tess: I helped write this story because almost all of my grandparents have had cancer, including my Nana Beverlye. Unfortunately, my Papa Lew passed away from lung cancer while we were writing this book, and I also lost my Grandma Ruth to cancer. Most of my friends don't know about cancer, so I thought with some research, Nana and I could explain it to them. I got the idea when I read my Nana's book *I Can Do This: Living with Cancer, Tracing a Year of Hope*. I have always written stories and reports, but never have published them. I hope that, from this book, you now understand that cancer is a hard disease and you can't do it alone. You must remember to always stay strong and give a loved one with cancer all your hope. Thanks a lot for reading this book. I hope it answered all your questions about cancer.

Acknowledgments

Thank you to the following people for their help, support, ideas, and continual faith in this project!

We give special thanks and appreciation to Terry Hamermesh because without her words of encouragement to her daughter and her unselfish commitment to this project, there would have been no book.

Thanks also to Editor Laura Taylor for her help and encouragement and to Cindy Martin, Jano Stack, Perie Longo, Susan Gulbransen, Bobbi Rosenblatt, Rita Rivest, and Richard Welna.

For their encouragement in this project, special thanks goes to Lois Capps, U. S. Congresswoman (CA); Dr. Jill Anter Wieder, psychologist; Dr. Charles Forscher, medical director of the Cedars-Sinai Sarcoma Center; and Dr. Daniel Greenfield, pediatric oncologist.

To Katie Welsh, Rachel Morrissey, Molly Wyer, and Megan Empey—we couldn't have done it without you! Editor Grace Rachow gave us a wonderful, helping hand and helped us reach the finish line with talent, patience, and humor.

Our thanks to Cindy Chang Salkin, Dr. Carolyn Bruzdzinski, Book Publishing Director Len Boswell, and Rebecca Teaff, our editor—all from the American Cancer Society. They all believed in us and made our book a reality.

This book was a family endeavor, so we give our biggest thanks to our family. Throughout the project, they have been our cheerleaders and our inspiration: Bob Fead; Jim Hyman and Leslie Weisberg Hyman and their sons, Gideon and Alexander; Terry Hamermesh; and Eric Hamermesh who provided expertise and many hours of help on legal matters.

—Beverlye and Tess

Glossary

abnormal: not normal. An abnormal lesion or growth may be cancerous, premalignant (likely to become cancer), or benign.

behavior: the way a person acts, or reacts, within his environment.

benign: not cancer; not malignant.

cancer: not just one disease but a group of diseases. All forms of cancer cause cells in the body to change and grow out of control. Most types of cancer cells form a lump or mass called a tumor. **cancerous** (*adj.*): related to or affected with cancer.

chemotherapy: treatment with drugs to destroy cancer cells. Chemotherapy is often used alone or with surgery or radiation, to treat cancer that has spread or come back.

diabetes: a disease in which the body does not properly control the amount of sugar in the blood.

diagnosis: the process of identifying a disease by its signs and symptoms and by using imaging tests and laboratory findings.

early detection: discovering a disease in the early stages.

environment: conditions, influences, or surroundings; the social and cultural forces that shape the life of a person or a population.

genetics: the study of genes and heredity. Heredity is the passing of genetic information and traits (such as eye color and an increased chance of getting a certain disease) from parents to offspring.

heart disease: any condition of the heart that impairs its functioning.

malignant: a mass of cells that may invade surrounding tissues or spread to distant areas of the body.

mammogram: an x-ray of the breast. Mammography is a method of finding breast cancer that can't be felt.

nutrition: the science of what people eat and drink and how it is digested and assimilated. Good nutrition consists of a balanced diet.

obesity: the condition of being very fat or overweight. Obesity is caused by a combination of bad eating habits and too little exercise.

oncologist: a doctor with special training in the diagnosis and treatment of cancer.

Pap test: this test involves scraping cells from a woman's cervix and looking at them under a microscope to see if abnormal cells are present. Also called a *Pap smear*.

pediatric oncologist: a doctor who specializes in cancers of children.

radiation therapy: treatment with high-energy rays (such as x-rays) to kill or shrink cancer cells. This is done with a special machine that gives radiation only to the part of the body that needs it.

screenings: the search for disease, in people without symptoms.

surgery: an operation or procedure to remove or repair a part of the body or to find out whether disease is present. Many tumors are removed with surgery, and the patient recovers and gets well.

survival rate: the percentage of people with a certain cancer who are alive for a certain period after diagnosis. For cancer patients, this is commonly expressed as five-year survival.

survivor: not generally used as a medical word, survivor can have several different meanings when applied to people with cancer. Some people use the word to refer to anyone who has been diagnosed with cancer. For example, someone living with cancer may be considered a survivor. Some people use the term when referring to one who has completed cancer treatment. And still others call a person a survivor if he or she has lived several years past a cancer diagnosis.

symptom: a change in the body caused by an illness, as described by the person experiencing it.

tissue: a group of cells that have a specific function.

tumor: an abnormal lump or mass of tissue. Tumors can be benign (non-cancerous) or malignant (cancerous).

x-ray: a form of radiation that can be used at low levels to produce an image of the body on film or at high levels to destroy cancer cells.

About the Authors

Photo by Dana Gluckstein

Beverlye Hyman Fead is an author, artist, poet, and cancer survivor. After an experimental treatment helped her survive stage IV cancer in 2002, she wrote the book *I Can Do This: Living with Cancer, Tracing a Year of Hope*. Beverlye frequently makes public appearances to share with others her inspiring story of courage and hope. She serves as an ambassador for the American Cancer Society's (ACS's) Celebration on the Hill™, a signature event that celebrates cancer survivorship and advocates for laws to help fight the disease. Beverlye has helped raise more than $1 million for cancer research and continues to be passionate for this cause. She also serves on the Community Council-Greater Santa Barbara Unit of the ACS in California and, in 2008, was named the Hero of Hope for the Silicon Coastal Region of the ACS. She received the 2009 Courage Award from the Sarcoma Foundation of America and has served as a member of the Board of Trustees at the Cancer Center of Santa Barbara. Beverlye resides in Santa Barbara, California, with her husband, music publisher Bob Fead. Beverlye and Bob have five grandchildren: Tess, Max, Alexander, Gideon, and Jackson.

Tessa Mae Hamermesh is eleven years old and the eldest of Beverlye's five grandchildren. Beverlye describes Tess as "the kind of girl who has at least a dozen incredible ideas every single day" and adds that this book was one of them. Tess enjoys reading, sports, and musical theatre. She participates in community service programs with her family and friends. Tess's goal is to help children her age learn more about cancer, as well as inspire them to participate in programs that are trying to stop cancer forever. In October 2008, Tess and Beverlye were keynote speakers at the annual fundraising luncheon of the Teddy Bear Cancer Foundation in Santa Barbara, California.

About the Illustrator

Shennen Bersani brings a unique blend of realism and heartfelt emotion to her art. As shown in her illustrations for *Nana, What's Cancer?* she is able to depict an exceptional likeness of her subjects. What further sets her work apart is the warmth and personality that shines through in every image.

Shennen's beautiful illustrations can be found in a variety of other well-known children's books, including *My Sister, Alicia May; Ocean Counting: Odd Numbers; Sharks: Big, Bigger, Biggest;* and *Snakes: Long, Longer, Longest.* She lives with her family near Boston, Massachusetts.